Printed and Published in Great Britain by D.C. Thomson &
Co. Ltd., 185 Fleet Street, London EC4A 2HS.

HIGH SCORE: 1937

COW PIE

COW PIE

SAY NO MORE, MR MAYOR! DESPERATE DAN WILL LEND A HAND!

SOME HARD WORK WILL KEEP MY MIND OFF FOOD!

SHAKE! SHUDDER!

WHAT'S GOING ON? IT SOUNDS LIKE THE MOUNTAIN IS ERUPTING!

IT'S JUST DAN HELPING OUT WITH THE TUNNEL!

NEARLY THERE, FOLKS!

DON'T YOU WANT A BREAK? SOMETHING TO EAT?

EAT? NOT WHILE THERE'S WORK TO BE DONE!

JAK and TODD

FIGHTING FOR YOUR RIGHT TO PARTY!

WHO'S THIS?

AH! THANKS FOR THE QUICK ANSWER!

YOU SWAPPED MY SHAMPOO FOR HAIR DYE AGAIN, DIDN'T YOU?

I CANNOT TELL A LIE...

YOU CAUGHT ME GREEN-HANDED!

I'VE TOLD YOU BEFORE, JAK - IF YOU CAN'T DYE YOUR SISTER'S HAIR A NICE COLOUR, DON'T DYE IT AT ALL!

I'M OFF TO SCHOOL - HAVE A NICE DYE... ER, DAY!

HAVE A NICE DAY? AT SCHOOL? FAT CHANCE!

OLLIE FLIPTRIK

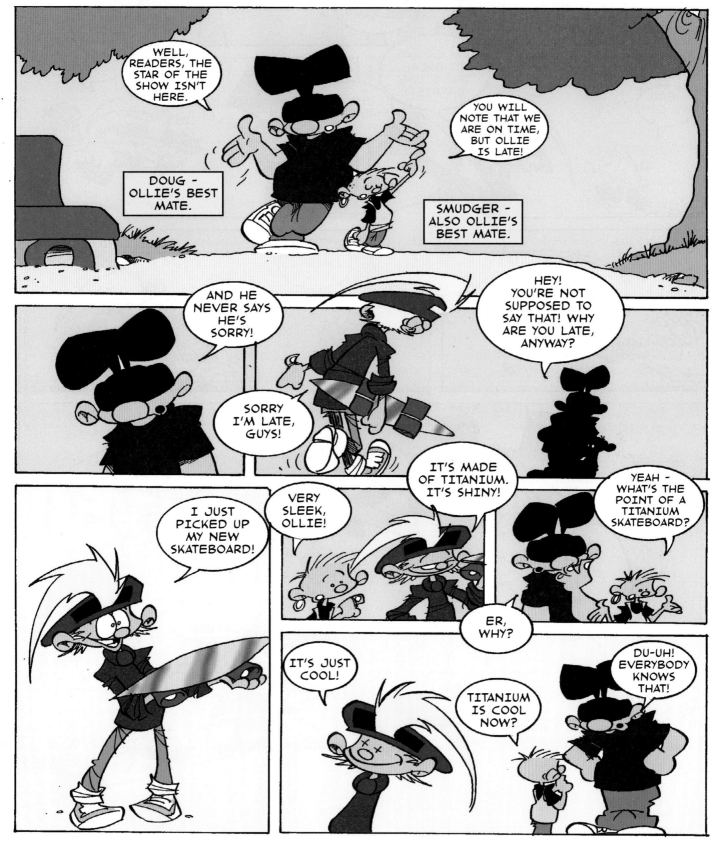

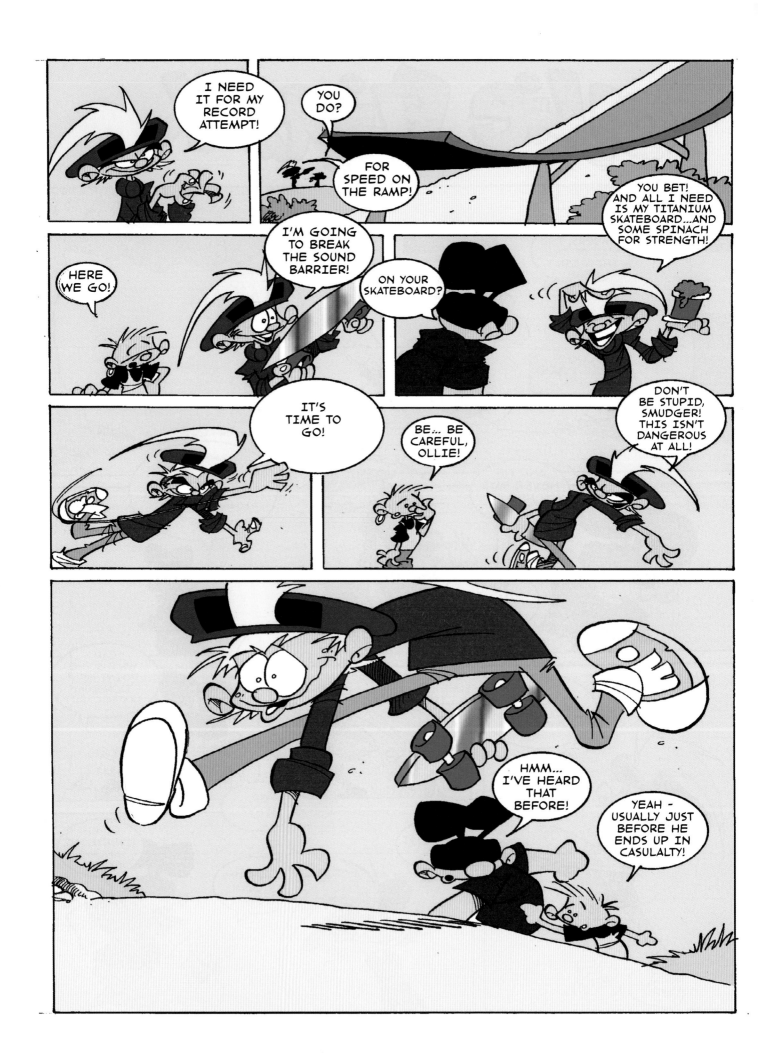

AGENTDOG2-ZERO

THIS IS AN ORDINARY HOUSE, ON AN ORDINARY STREET...

AND THIS IS JUST AN ORDINARY DOG CHASING AN ORDINARY CAT...

HOLD IT RIGHT THERE, AGENT DOG 2 ZERO!

WAIT A MINUTE! THIS ISN'T ORDINARY!

OKAY, MR TIDDLES! I'LL DO AS YOU SAY!

SAY, IS THAT A SUPER-ATOMIC NUCLEAR WIPEOUT GUN?

YES, IT IS! ISN'T SHE A BEAUTY!

I HAD IT MADE SPECIALLY FOR ME. WOULD YOU LIKE TO HOLD IT?

DON'T MIND IF I DO...

OH, THAT'S NICE...

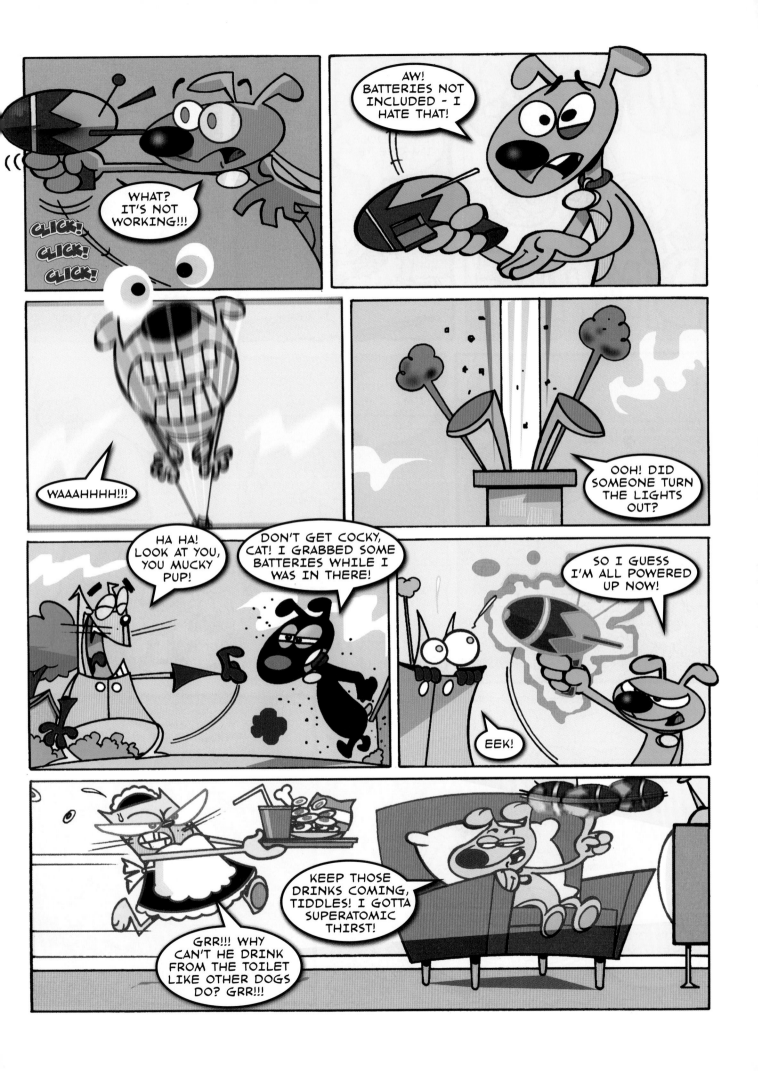

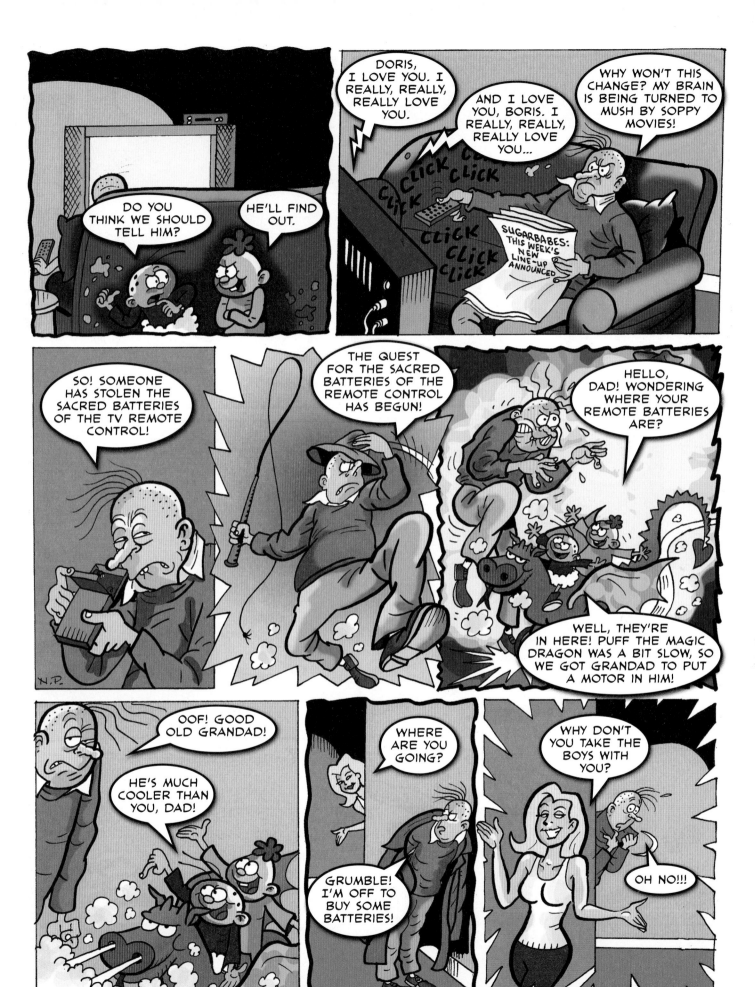

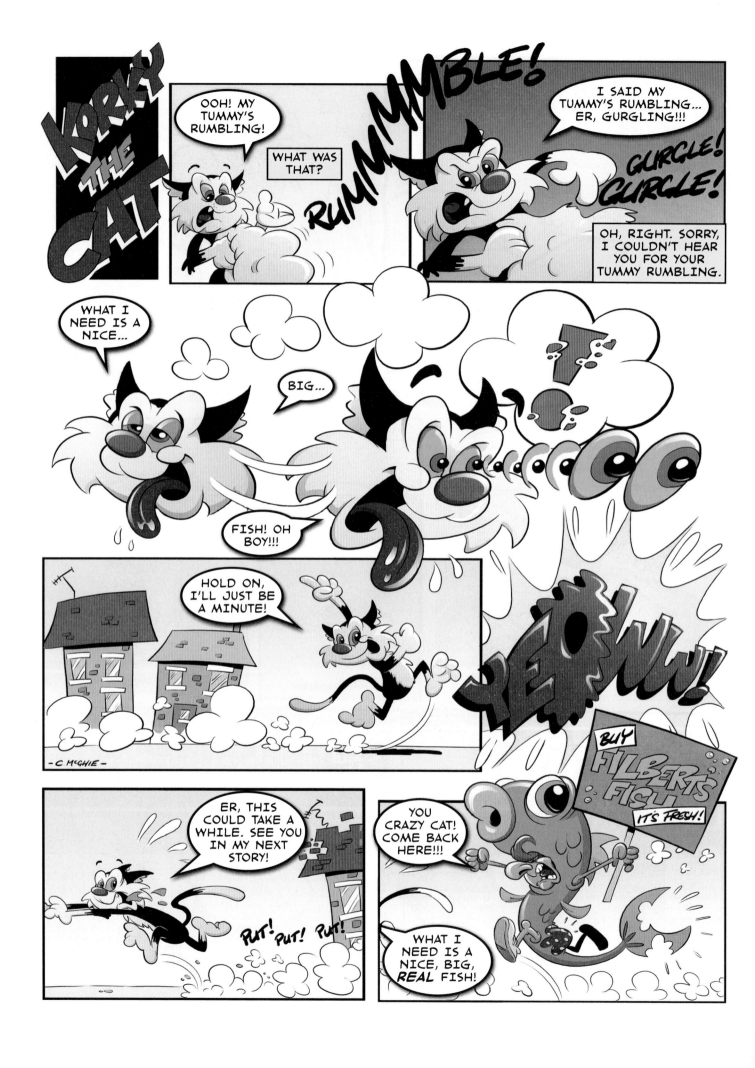

DESPERATE DAN

CACTUSVILLE, IN THE WILD WEST. THIS A TOUGH PLACE FOR TOUGH MEN. TOUGH MEN, LIKE...

SHAVE

HARDWARE STORE

SALOO

JAIL

SHERIFF KURT DIDDLEY?

WHAT'S WRONG, SHERIFF?

IT'S THE CLANTONS, DAN!

THEY'VE BEEN CATTLE-RUSTLING AND I JUST CAN'T STOP THEM! I DON'T HAVE TIME TO TRACK DOWN ALL OF THEM!

THE CLANTONS, EH?

LEAVE IT TO ME! I CAN SORT THOSE CATTLE-RUSTLIN' LOSERS OUT FOR YOU!

OH, THANKS DAN!

NOW, HOW TO CATCH A RUSTLER? WHAT WOULD LURE A RUSTLER INTO GETTING CAUGHT?

SO—

ER, MOOOOOOO!!!

THIS WILL FOOL THOSE CLANTONS INTO GETTING CLOSE TO ME, I RECKON!

GOOD WORK!

THE SHERIFF IS GONNA BE MIGHTY PLEASED WITH ME!!!

Here are the words to find! Cowboy, Cowpie, Cactus, Bandit, Injuns, Dawg, Zeke, Sheriff, Cactusville, Ravine, Saloon, Rattlesnake, Grizzly, Pig, Beans, Lasso, Howdy

PUZZLE 1:
Cap'n Orangebeard's pirate flag is all torn up, but there seem to be more pieces of it than he needs. Can you tell which is one piece too many?

ARRRRR!
These three rubbish pirates have gotten caught in a whirlpool, can you help them out?

Puzzle 2:
Someone's treasure fell overboard, how many coins can you find floating around?

Puzzle 3:
Cap'n Greenbeard fell into the whirlpool! Can you guide him back up to his ship?

Puzzle 4:
Cap'n Redbeard's treasure is hidden on an island nearby, but in which direction is it? Work out the letters from the clues, then rearrange them to find out!

North, South, East or West? Here be clues...
My first is in TREE but not in BARK,
My second OUTSIDE but not in the DARK,
My third is in SEA but not in SAW,
My last isn't in FIGHT, but always in WAR!

JAMIE SMART

AGENT DOG 2-ZERO

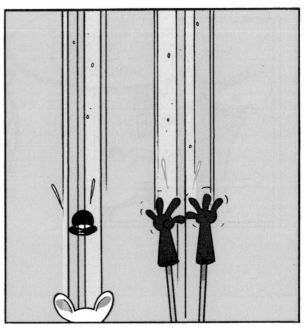

MARVO THE WONDER CHICKEN!

IN "AN ARROW ESCAPE!"

BULLY BEEF & CHIPS

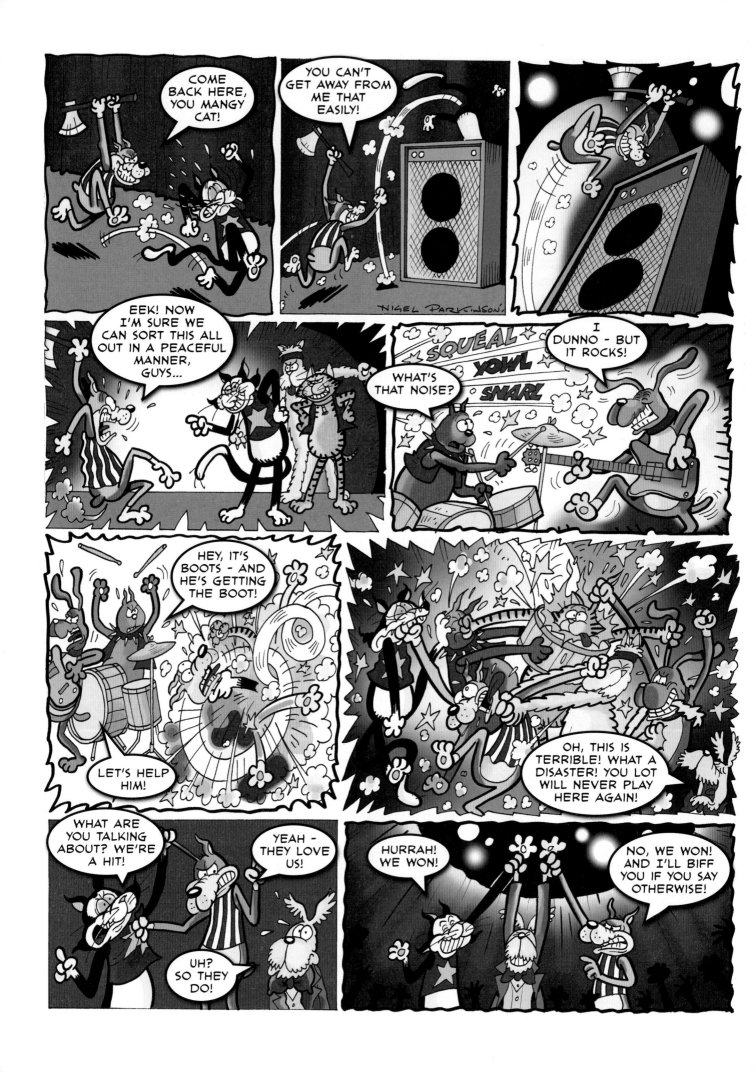

JAK and TODD

FIGHTING FOR *YOUR* RIGHT TO PARTY!

CAR BOOT SALES ARE A GREAT WAY TO SELL SOME OF YOUR STUFF!

THAT'S NOT WHAT WE'RE DOING!

WE'RE SELLING SOMEONE ELSE'S STUFF!

MY BIG SISTER MANDY'S STUFF, TO BE PRECISE!

AND SHE DOESN'T KNOW!

LOOK! HERE COMES A SALE!

YOU LOOK LIKE YOU COULD DO WITH SOME HELP FOR YOUR HAIR, MADAM! THESE FRIZZ-AWAY HAIR TONGS WILL GET RID OF THOSE HORRIBLE FRIZZY BITS...

SHUT UP, DUDE! SHE'S LOSING IT!

ARE YOU SAYING I HAVE HORRIBLE HAIR?

ER, NO! HAVE THESE TONGS ANYWAY... FOR FREE... AND PLEASE DON'T KILL ME!

JAK!

EEP! BUSTED!

YOU THOUGHT YOU'D GOT AWAY WITH IT, DIDN'T YOU?

I DON'T KNOW WHAT YOU'RE TALKING ABOUT!

YOU FORGOT MY CHANGE.

SO WE DID. PAY THE MAN, TODD.

WITH PLEASURE! SORRY, SIR!

WE'RE SOLD OUT!

WHAT ELSE CAN WE SELL?

WE'RE GOING FOR A BURGER - WANT SOMETHING?

NO, THANKS!

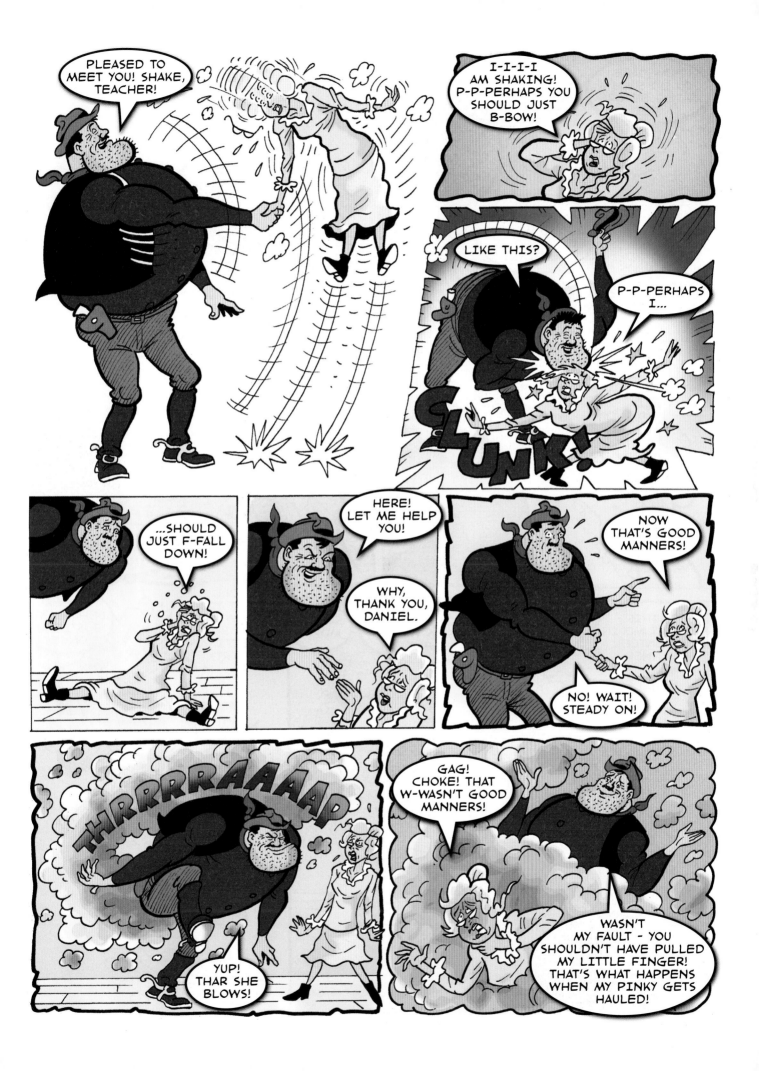

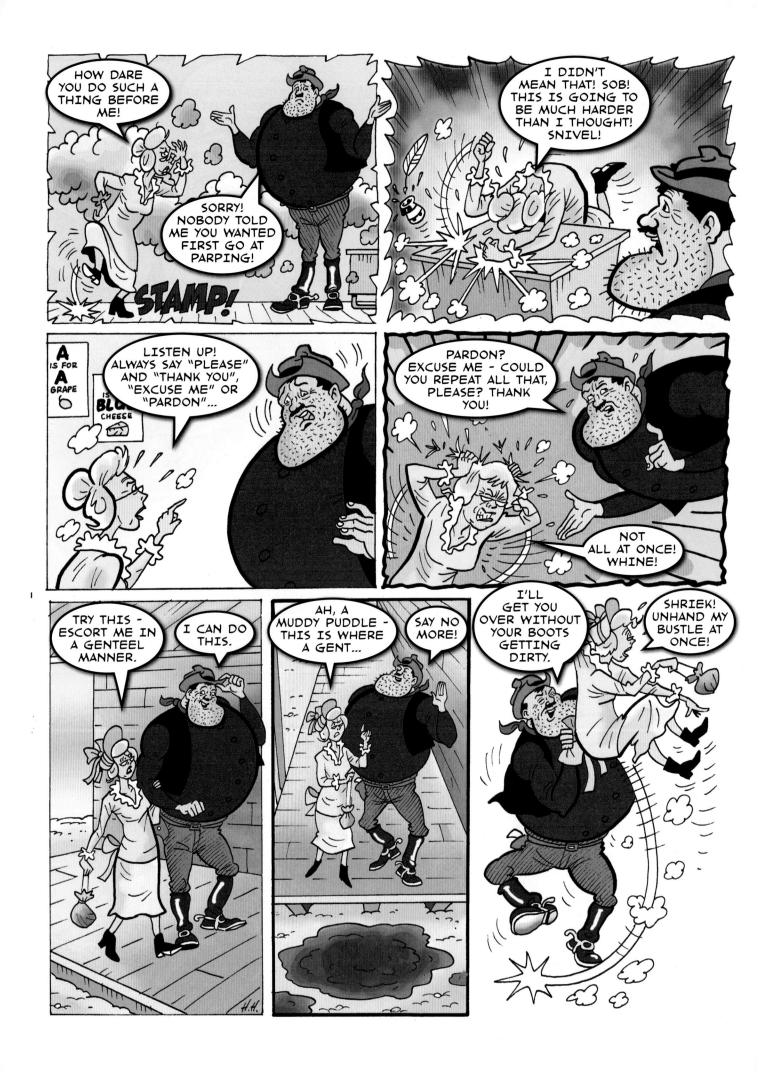

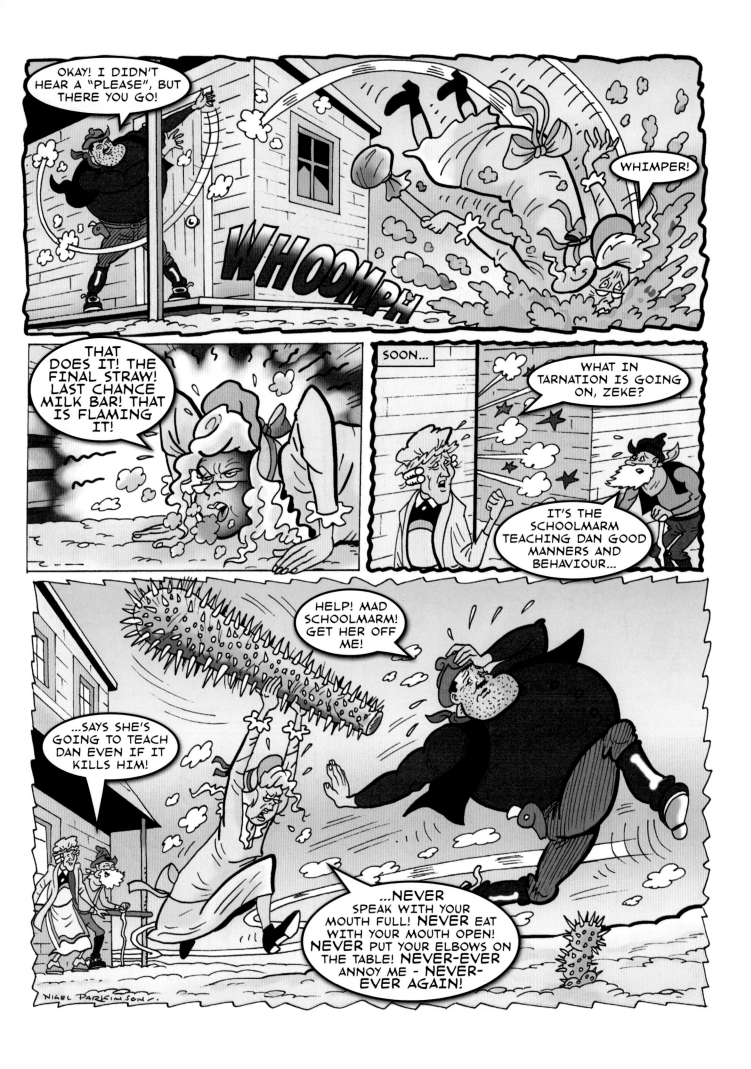

JAK and TODD
FIGHTING FOR YOUR RIGHT TO PARTY!

IT'S PARENTS' NIGHT TONIGHT. IS YOUR MUM GOING?

MY MUM GOES TO EVERYTHING, DUDE. JUST LIKE YOUR FOLKS.

I WONDER IF THERE'S WAY TO STOP THEM GOING - IF THEY GET CHATTING WITH OUR TEACHER OR THE HEAD, WE'LL BE GROUNDED TILL EASTER!

DUDE - WE ARE GOING TO MAKE A MOVIE!

OKAY, THAT'S THE FOOTAGE OF THE SCHOOL WE NEED.

NOW FOR THE SPECIAL EFFECTS!

WE CAN JUST PATCH IT RIGHT INTO THE AERIAL AND HEY, PRESTO! THE SIX O'CLOCK NEWS, JAK AND TODD STYLEE!

AND NOW FOR LOCAL NEWS. AN EXPLOSION HAS ROCKED MIDDLETON ACADEMY...

HONEY, THE KIDS' SCHOOL IS ON TV!

BANANAMAN

YOU CAN PAY FOR IT, THEN!

OH, MOTHER! I DON'T THINK I HAVE ANY MONEY!

I'VE GOT 5 PENCE. WHAT CAN I GET FOR THAT?

HERE YOU GO!

EUGH!

YUCK!

FAZ-PFAPT!

CRUMBS! THAT OVER-RIPE BANANA HAS TURNED ME INTO AN OVER-RIPE SUPERHERO!

MUST CATCH THAT CROOK!

OWEN GOAL

NIGEL PARKINSON.

MARVO THE WONDER CHICKEN!

"THE FRIGHT BEFORE CHRISTMAS PART ONE!"

AGENT DOG 2-ZERO

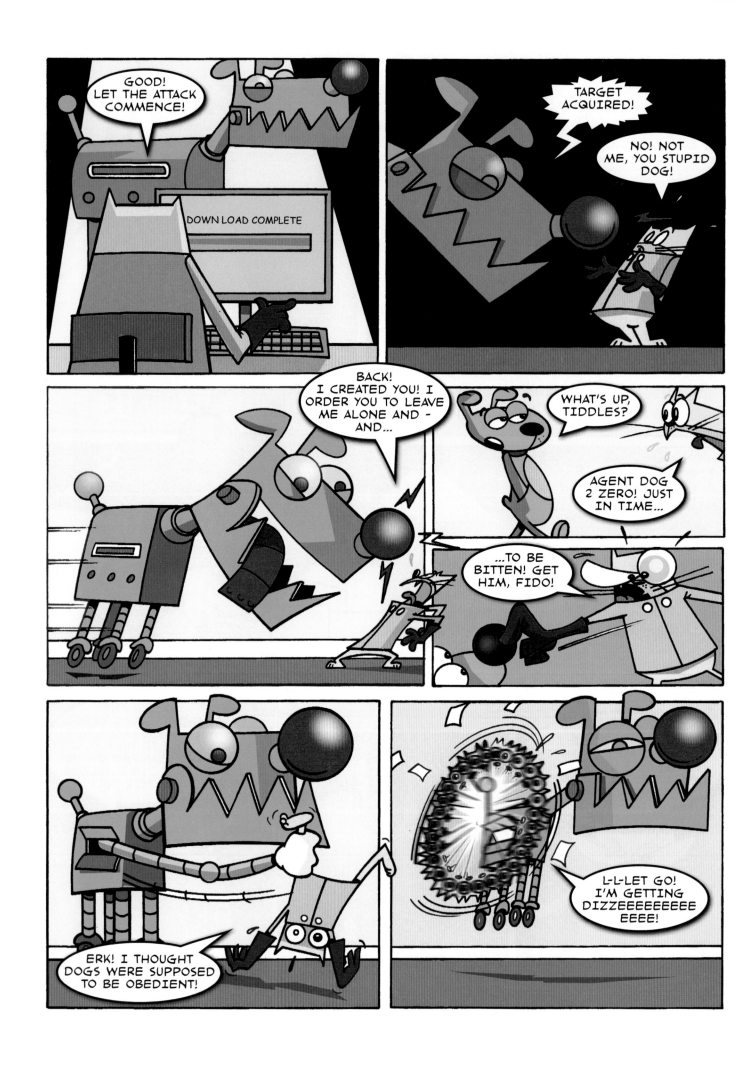

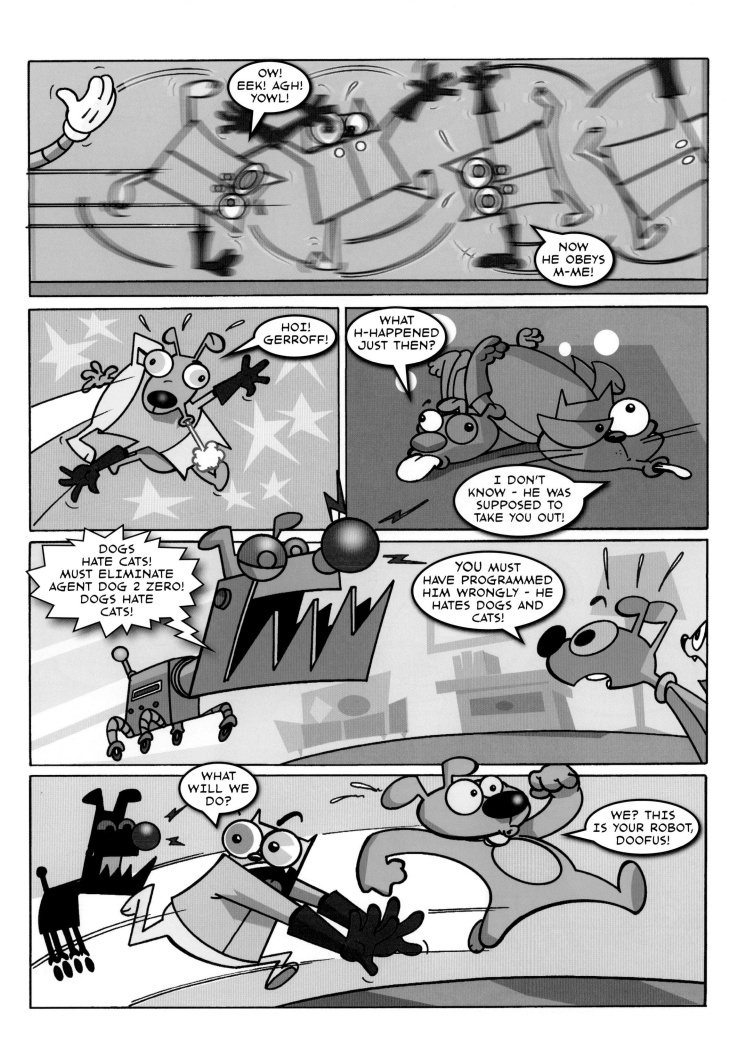

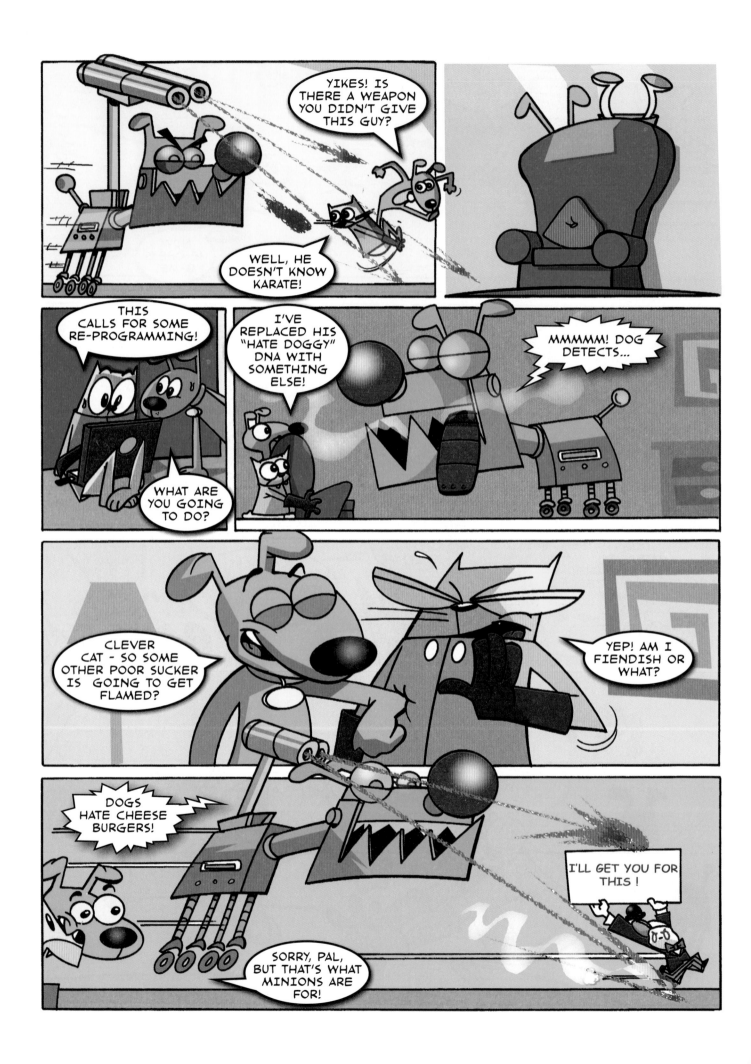

DESPERATE DAN'S COLUMN, EH? BUT NOBODY COULD SEE ME FROM THE GROUND IF I WAS TOO HIGH UP.

NAH – THAT IDEA'S FOR THE BIRDS, MAYOR!

WELL, WE COULD PUT A PLAQUE UP TO CELEBRATE YOUR LIFE!

THIS PLAQUE COMMEMORATES THE DAY STINKY STAN WASHED HIS PANTS 1843

SHERIFF, THAT'S JUST PLAIN DULL!

WELL, WE'LL JUST HAVE TO BUILD A STATUE!

OUR BELOVED MAYOR (SIGN PAID FOR BY THE MAYOR)

THERE'S NOTHING LIKE A GOOD STATUE ... AND THAT IS NOTHING LIKE A GOOD STATUE! I'M NOT TAKING A CHANCE WITH MY LIKENESS!